D1187992

17.

-2

16

16

WOODLANDS

314418

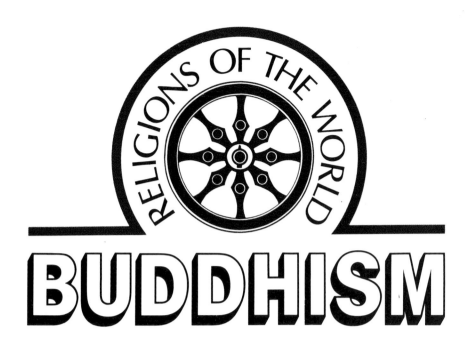

RELIGIONS OF THE WORLD

BUDDHISM

John Snelling

Religions of the World

Buddhism
Christianity
Hinduism
Islam
Judaism
Sikhism

First published in 1986 by
Wayland (Publishers) Limited
61 Western Road, Hove
East Sussex BN3 1JD, England

©Copyright 1986 Wayland (Publishers) Limited

British Library Cataloguing in Publication Data
Snelling, John
Buddhism. — (Religions of the world (Wayland))
1. Buddhism — Juvenile literature
I. Title   II. Series
294.3   BQ4032

ISBN 0-85078-722-X

Photoset by Planagraphic Typesetters Limited
Printed and bound in Italy by Sagdos S.p.A.

Contents

The Origins of Buddhism

Have you ever gone off alone — for a walk in the countryside, maybe, or just up to your room — and suddenly become aware of how strange and wonderful everything is? In fact, you may start to think how incredible it is that there should be a world at all, let alone a world full of so many varied and beautiful things. Why isn't there just nothingness, or grey swirling cloud? Or just a meaningless mess? Who made it all, and why?

If we then consider ourselves, we find a greater mystery still. Who is this person called 'I' that is looking out at the world?

Buddhists find that being alone helps their concentration.

Where does this person come from? Take a look at yourself when you have got a quiet moment to spare. Do you really know who you are?

Usually if someone asks us what religion is about, we think of churches, mosques, temples, synagogues, prayers, hymns, and so on. But these things come second. All the great religions of the world in fact started with some remarkable person who went off alone and began to ask very searching questions, like the ones mentioned above. But not only did they ask questions; they came up with some answers too.

Siddhartha Gautama

Siddhartha Gautama was one of these remarkable people. History tells us that he was born the son of a king in northern India about 2,500 years ago. As you can imagine, his early life was one of luxury and privilege. He lived in fantastic palaces, enjoying the best food, clothing and entertainments. This good life, however, was not enough for Gautama; he wanted to know what the rest of the world was like. So he began to go off in his chariot to visit the village near his palace. What he found there was like nothing he had ever known. He saw poor people, sick people, and even dead bodies being carried off to be cremated.

These discoveries so horrified Gautama that he could enjoy palace life no longer. He longed to find out whether there was a way of ending suffering.

Above *All the great religions began not with ceremonies and services, but with simple human experience.*

Below *A frieze showing the young prince being driven in his chariot.*

A modern Indian holy man, or sadhu.

The quest

Determined to answer this question, he slipped out of his palace one night, leaving his wife and young baby behind, and took the road to the next kingdom. As soon as he had crossed the frontier river, he took off his gorgeous silk robe and put on one of patched and faded orange cloth. He cut off all his fine, jet-black hair and gave his rings and ornaments to the servant who had come to the frontier with him. Then, carrying nothing but a simple begging-bowl into which kind people could if they wished put food for him, he said goodbye to his servant and set off in search of an answer to his great question. He was no longer Prince Siddhartha, but just a penniless holy man.

In India there have always been men who have given up everything in order to go off into lonely places and search for truth. Gautama in his day sought out the most famous of them and begged them to teach him all that they knew. He studied very hard under them and also performed various exercises, rather like yoga exercises, which were supposed to help him see the truth. It is said that he lived in terrifying forests, burning in the heat of the midday sun and freezing at night, and that he slept on beds of thorns. He also starved himself until his body became so weak and thin that if he touched his stomach, he could feel his backbone poking through from the other side.

He did not, however, find an answer

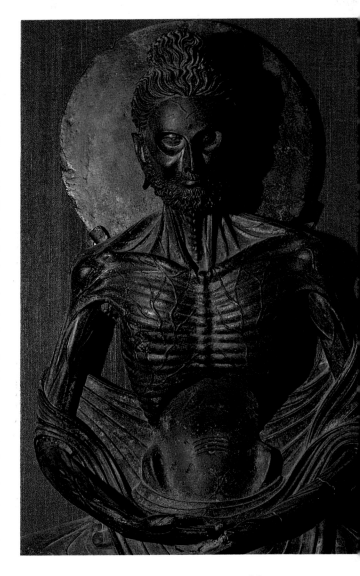

Gautama almost starved himself to death on his quest for truth.

to his basic question. Moreover, he realized that if he went on treating his body as he had been, he wouldn't live much longer. He therefore took a little food to give him strength, whereupon the other holy men that had been his friends promptly declared that 'Gautama has taken to the luxurious life' and left him.

The Buddha

Enlightenment

Alone and forsaken now, Gautama realized that he had to carry on his quest by himself. He came to a place nowadays called Budh Gaya, where he found a huge Bo tree. Making himself a cushion of grass beneath the tree, he determined to sit there until he found an answer to his question.

Now, instead of looking outside himself, Gautama lowered his eyelids and began to look within. He saw thoughts, feelings, memories, sensations, desires, fears and much else besides. As he watched them, he began to see how these powerful forces, working together, created the idea of the person Gautama — the person he himself identified as 'I'.

When he looked more closely, however, where was this Gautama, this 'I'? He could certainly trace shifting, unstable patterns of feeling and thought, but no fixed and unchanging soul or self. In fact there was nothing — but not an empty, meaningless nothing. It was indeed a powerful reality, something that was in everything.

This reality was not subject to change, nor could it be rocked by the emotions. As it had never been born into the world, it could not die, so Gautama called it 'the deathless', or *nirvana*, a relaxed state of being in which

A magnificent temple now stands at Budh Gaya in northern India.

there was no grasping after anything. Most of all, it could not be affected by suffering, so it was precisely what Gautama had set out to find.

Legend has it that Siddhartha's final understanding, or 'enlightenment', came after the night of the full moon of May. As dawn broke, he looked up and saw the morning star rising. At that moment he saw the truth for himself. He was Gautama no more, but the *Buddha*, or 'Awakened One'.

Turning the wheel of Dharma

At first the Buddha was not at all keen to tell other people about his great discovery. He thought that they wouldn't want to know. But then he was persuaded that there were some who had 'just a little dust in their eyes'. These people might, with a little assistance, be helped to see the truth.

Representations of the Buddha's nirvana *often seek to show the calmness and serenity which came to him at that time.*

9

He therefore went to Isipatana (modern Sarnath, near Benares in northern India), where he delivered a sermon to a small crowd in the deer park there. As the Buddha's teaching is called the *Dharma* and is often symbolized by an eight-spoked wheel, this first sermon is celebrated as the occasion upon which he 'first turned the wheel of the *Dharma*'.

A sculpture of the Buddha delivering a sermon to his followers.

This was the beginning of a great forty-five year period during which the Buddha walked the dusty roads of northern India, spreading his message among the people. He taught without caring about which class, race or sex his listeners belonged to. Some of his

10

Monks and lay people mingle at a ceremony in Ladakh, northern India.

followers were householders: people with jobs and homes. Others, however, were prepared to give up everything like that in order to devote themselves entirely to listening to the Buddha's teaching and putting it into practice. These people eventually became known as the *sangha,* the community of Buddhist monks and nuns. From the start, they were supported entirely by lay people. They just wandered from place to place, accepting gifts of food and drink from the people. Later, monasteries were built in which they could live together as a community for at least part of the year.

Parinirvana

The Buddha was a very remarkable person, but he was not a god or a superman of any sort. He was a human being with the same problems and limitations as the rest of us. He therefore had to die at some stage.

His death in fact took place as the result apparently of some kind of food poisoning, in a small town in northern India called Kushinagara. His last message to his followers was: 'Impermanent are all compounded things. Strive on mindfully.' He then passed into what Buddhists call his *parinirvana.* His first *nirvana* at Budh Gaya had been a kind of death to self; his *parinirvana,* then, involved something more — death of the body as well. What actually became of the Buddha after the death of his body is a great mystery. It is something that is beyond the mind of ordinary man to know and of words to tell.

11

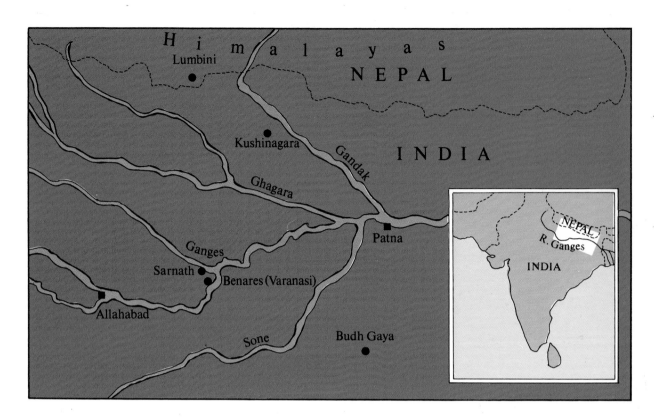

Above *The area of north-eastern India in which the Buddha spent nearly all his life.*

Below *This massive statue of the Buddha's* parinirvana *is in Sri Lanka.*

Teachings of the Buddha

The Buddha didn't want to give people something to believe in, nor to comfort them in their lives on earth. He felt that they should not depend upon others, not even upon himself. He simply wanted people to see the truth for themselves, just as he had seen it. Anything else was second-hand and second-best, and could all too easily be twisted around.

Consider what it would be like if you had spent all your life in a desert, far from the coast, and someone tried to describe the sea to you. They would of course tell you about the waves and the fish, but at the end of it all, you might be left with quite the wrong idea. If, however, you went to the seaside yourself, you could see, smell and feel the ocean, and you would be left in no doubt as to what it was like. You would know, directly from your own personal experience.

The Buddha did give teachings for his followers to use, but only to help them to find the truth for themselves. He also suggested a number of practical things, including meditation, that people could do for themselves.

Rock paintings in Tibet. Pure Buddhism is not really about gods, but the religion has fostered its own popular mythology.

The Middle Way

The Buddha taught what is called 'the Middle Way', a path that avoids all extremes. He had himself once lived a life of great luxury, as we have seen, before taking the opposite course and punishing his body. He eventually found the truth by following a path that ran between these two extremes.

On reflection, he realized that there was a useful pointer in this experience. He saw that when we get one-sided, when we start to concentrate too much on one single course of action, then invariably we are beginning to head off course.

Below *Buddhist art tends to depict the Buddha in a comfortable, but never luxurious environment.*

Above *Monks at Borobodur.*

Suffering

'Suffering I teach and the way out of suffering' — the Buddha.

As we have seen, the Buddha did not set out to discover the meaning of life, or the creator of the universe or anything like that. He started with the plain fact that all human beings suffer, although the usual word that Buddhists use, *dukkha*, implies something wider than what we understand by suffering. *Dukkha* has for Buddhists a sense of general unsatisfactoriness, a feeling that 'things are never quite right for me'.

This statue of the Buddha shows the calmness of nirvana.

The Buddha's first sermon, at Isipatana, was in fact all about suffering. In that sermon he listed what he called The Four Noble Truths:

1. Suffering exists.
2. The cause of suffering.
3. The cause may be ended.
4. The means whereby this can be done: by following The Noble Eightfold Path.

The root cause of suffering is the

15

mechanism of desire, or grasping, that has been placed in us all. This mechanism, working through our thoughts and emotions, is continually striving to build up the sense of 'I' within us. It creates the idea of a self, this person here that stands against the rest of the world. The self wants what is pleasurable and hangs on like mad when it gets it.

To move away from suffering, to break its hold over us, the Buddha taught that we must somehow loosen the power of grasping within us. At the same time we must begin to let go of our obsession with 'I', 'me' and 'mine'.

Below *The Buddhist Wheel of Life. On the outside of the wheel is Mara, the Lord of Time. Everything inside the wheel is conditioned; subject to time, and death.*

Opposite *Laity prepare a meal for monks. By giving, people can restrain their self-interest.*

The Life of a Buddhist

The Noble Eightfold Path

The Buddha believed that people could escape from suffering by following certain principles:

1. Right seeing or understanding
2. Right thought
3. Right speech
4. Right action
5. Right livelihood
6. Right effort
7. Right mindfulness
8. Right contemplation

These principles he called The Noble Eightfold Path, and Buddhists try to practise as many of them as they can. The first step, 'right seeing', involves accepting the basic truth of the Buddha's teachings before any attempt is made to put them into practice. This is important, because if a person sets out to follow the Buddha's way with a completely false idea of it's true nature, then things are likely to go very wrong.

The next four steps are all about trying to live a good life by not lying, stealing, committing violent or destructive

A Tibetan monk studies religious scriptures: 'right seeing' is the first step on the Eightfold Path.

acts, or earning a living in an immoral way, such as by selling guns or products that are either useless or harmful to people. We in the West call these kinds of principles 'morality'; Buddhists call them *sila*. For Buddhists, *sila* is not so much a matter of setting up laws that you should not break, as of having ideals to shape your conduct. Living this

The basic conditions in which monks live are designed to curb the demands of the self.

way, you not only make life easier for others, but you also restrain grasping and desire in yourself. If you think about it, nearly all so-called immoral actions stem from wanting something

19

Being a Buddhist is very much about active participation in the religion.

for yourself. Stealing, for instance —
except in cases of genuine hardship —
usually stems from greed. By restraining
greed, you reduce the power of 'I' within
yourself and bring into play that deeper
level of being, or *nirvana,* that the Buddha himself discovered as he sat alone
beneath the Bo tree at Budh Gaya.

'Right effort' comes next in the
Eightfold Path because Buddhism is
very much about doing something for
oneself. It is not good enough for a person to say 'I am a Buddhist', and then sit
back and expect everything to happen
of its own accord. He or she has got to
use a little energy and work at being a
good Buddhist.

'Right mindfulness' and 'right contemplation' are methods that can be

*A Japanese Zen Buddhist in
meditation. Gardens such as this one
encourage calmness of mind, and
'right contemplation'.*

used to increase one's wisdom. The first
involves trying to be aware of everything
that is going on both outside oneself
and, more importantly, inside oneself.
If you think about it, you realize that
many people spend their lives in a state
of semi-sleep, even when they're up and
about. They simply do not observe what
is going on around them. Fewer people
still look within themselves to find out
about their own true nature. They are
just too caught up in all the thoughts
and feelings that are whirling about in
their heads.

21

A giant statue of the Buddha in Colombo, Sri Lanka.

22

'Right contemplation' involves meditation, which is such an important part of Buddhism that it should be explained in more detail.

Meditation

Statues of the Buddha, like the one on the preceding page, show him in meditation. Buddhists meditate to help themselves come to a deeper understanding of the Buddha's teaching.

How do they go about it? Firstly, they usually sit upright, with their heads erect and backs straight, either on a chair or cross-legged on the floor. They then lower their eyelids, without closing them altogether, and look inside their own minds. They may at first use some kind of technique, such as counting each breath, to help them with their concentration.

The first step in meditation is to calm the mind. If you look within yourself, you will see that your mind is abuzz with thoughts and feelings. You may be remembering last night's television programmes or looking forward to what you're going to have for lunch. Your mind, in fact, is always full of desires and thoughts, which get in the way of 'right contemplation'. Eventually all these things begin to calm down, and fade away. The mind becomes calm and clear. In some ways the mind is rather like a deep lake. It's all waves and turmoil on the surface, but as you go deeper, things become calmer. You find

Dedicated monks spend as much time in meditation as possible.

great spaciousness there, and peace. You are now reaching those levels of the mind that the Buddha discovered below the chaos and clutter of the surface. Only then do you realize that this haven of calm has been in the background all along, without you ever having noticed it. It could be said that you have come back to the home you never left.

The Buddhist Philosophy

The Three Fires

'Your house is on fire. It burns with the Three Fires. There is no dwelling in it.' — The Buddha in his Fire Sermon.

The house that the Buddha was speaking about is the human body; the three fires that are burning in it are the fires of greed, hatred, and ignorance.

The Buddha didn't divide the human race into good people and bad people. He taught that all people have both good and bad, light and dark sides to them. Many people, however, don't like their dark side and so they try to sweep it under the carpet, concentrating instead upon their virtues and good points. Unfortunately, the bad side of oneself doesn't just go away if it is ignored. In fact, disregarded, it is quite likely to influence our behaviour in all kinds of unpleasant ways.

A Buddhist, therefore, uses the practice of mindfulness to increase his or her awareness of all aspects of the self. In this way, the dark side of the personality will be brought into the light and transformed. Then the powerful energies that fuel greed, hatred and ignorance can be turned into forces for good.

The cock, snake and boar at the centre of the Wheel of Life symbolize greed, hatred and ignorance respectively.

The Three Signs of Being

The Buddha taught that everything that exists is subject to three things: change (*anicca*), suffering (*dukkha*) and something he called *anatta*. He called these universal conditions the Three Signs of Being.

Change is not difficult to see. Everything is in the process of moving on; nothing stays the same, not even ourselves. We are not the same people that we were ten minutes ago, let alone ten years ago. Different ideas fill our minds, different emotions rule our hearts; even our bodies have changed in size and character: old cells have died, new ones have been made.

We have already dealt with suffering *(dukkha)*, but *anatta* is a little more difficult for non-Buddhists to understand. For all our surface changes, most of us tend to think that there is something permanent and unchanging within ourselves. We call this 'I' or the self. If we believe in some form of life after death, it is this that leaves our bodies at the final hour and lives on. As we have seen, however, when he looked deep within himself beneath the Bo tree at Budh Gaya, the Buddha could not find this permanent self. It simply was not there. All that was there was unstable and impermanent. *Anatta* points to this fact, the fact of our own nothingness. The Buddha saw these Three Signs of Being as defining all forms of earthly existence.

Buddhism does not separate humanity into believers and non-believers; tolerance is a highly respected virtue. Here His Holiness the Dalai Lama, the leader of Tibetan Buddhists, meets with the Dean of Westminster.

Offerings before a statue of Ananda, one of the Buddha's disciples. The idea of karma *endows such offerings with a special significance.*

Karma and rebirth

The Buddha taught that everything is conditioned; that is, it is caused by something else. And that cause was in turn caused by a previous cause, and so on back into time immemorial.

This means that when we do something in a deliberate way, this action is somehow going to reflect back upon us. If our motivation was bad — if we acted out of greed, hatred or ignorance — then the comeback is likely to be negative. On the other hand, if our motivation was good, it produces merit and the return will be a positive one. This process of cause and effect is called *karma* by Buddhists.

Closely connected with this is the idea of rebirth. This is often confused with reincarnation, which is the view that when we die, we somehow pass into a new body and so live a countless number of lives. In Buddhism, however, there is no permanent, unchanging 'I', as we have already seen. There is just a pattern of ever-changing conditions, so there is nothing permanent to reincarnate. Buddhists believe however, that we are all being born again from moment to moment. We are part of a causal chain: what we are today influences what we are tomorrow, and so on, even after death. A *buddha*, however, is someone who has managed to get off this eternally whirling merry-go-round: he is free at last, no longer subject to rebirth.

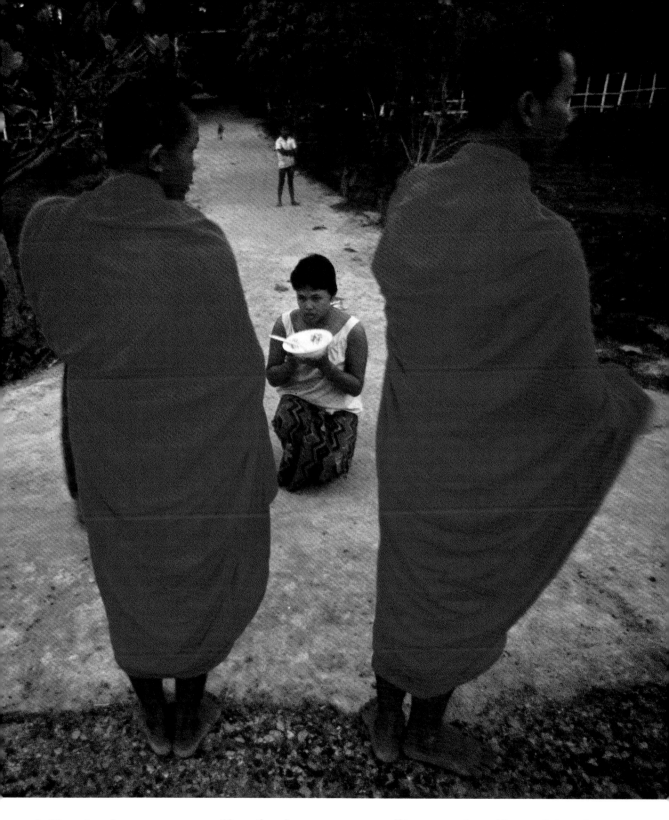

A Kampuchean woman offers food to some travelling monks. Alms-giving is considered a good way of gaining merit.

Compassion

'Not to do evil, to cultivate the good and to purify one's heart — this is the teaching of the buddhas.'

As we have seen, Buddhists place wisdom, or knowledge of who we really are, first and foremost. Once we have this knowledge and are free of enslavement to notions of 'I' and 'me', then we begin to see the world differently. We

The monastic life helps monks develop virtues such as compassion.

no longer see it as divided up into millions of individual units all set against each other, but rather as one interrelated whole. To a Buddhist the universe is one undivided whole, made up of harmonious interlinking parts. When we realize the true nature of the universe, we rediscover our basic brotherhood with all other beings and their pain and suffering are felt as our own. Thus, although Buddhists value such virtues as patience, humility, generosity and kindness very highly, they consider compassion the greatest virtue of all.

Not harming other beings

If suffering is unpleasant for ourselves, it must also be unpleasant for other beings too, and by 'other beings' Buddhists don't mean just humans, but animals, birds and even insects as well. It is an essential part of the Buddhist way of life not to cause suffering to other beings.

This compassionate desire has prompted many Buddhists to become pacifists — people who don't want to have anything to do with war. Others have become vegetarians and have cut meat out of their diets entirely because, of course, animals have to be slaughtered in order to provide us with meat. But Buddhists are not obliged to be vegetarian. They can, if they like, buy meat from a shop and eat it, as long as an animal has not been killed specially to feed them.

Buddhist monks conduct a ceremony at the London Peace Pagoda.

A group of monks being served a simple meal.

The Buddhist Community

Buddhism around the world

Buddhism, as we have seen, began in northern India, and from there it spread to other parts of the sub-continent. In the second century BC, the Emperor Aśoka, then the most powerful man in India, made Buddhism his own religion. Legend has it that he was deeply disturbed by the enormous numbers of people killed in a war he waged against a neighbouring people called the Kalingas. He was perhaps attracted to Buddhism because of its emphasis on compassion and non-violence.

A procession of monks in Sri Lanka, which has the oldest continuous Buddhist tradition in the world.

The religion later fell into decline in India, but by then it had already established itself elsewhere. In the country we today call Sri Lanka, the people were converted to Buddhism by a missionary called Mahinda, the son of the Emperor Aśoka. Burma, Thailand and Kampuchea also embraced Buddhism, as did some of the people in other parts of South East Asia. The form of Buddhism practised in these southern Asian countries is called Theravada Buddhism, Theravada meaning 'the Way of the Elders'.

Monks of the Theravada school can be identified by their orange robes.

The other major form of the religion is called Mahayana Buddhism, which means 'the Great Way'. It was once followed by people in Nepal, Sikkim, Bhutan, Tibet, Mongolia, Vietnam, Korea and Japan, and is still an important religion in some of these places.

The two forms of Buddhism differ from each other quite significantly. The followers of the Theravada take the *arahat* as their ideal. *Arahats* are people who have found salvation for themselves by reaching *nirvana*, that deathless state which the Buddha himself achieved.

Mahayanan monks conduct a New Year ceremony in India.

Mahayanists, on the other hand, adhere to the ideal of the *bodhisattva*, the wise person who has found *nirvana*, but who out of warm-hearted compassion for the suffering of other beings, puts off his own salvation in order to stay in the world and help others.

Unfortunately, war, politics and the influence of foreign cultures have had a damaging effect on the Buddhist religion in many parts of Asia. On the

31

Above *Monks outside a pagoda in Kew Gardens, London.*

The sangha

From the earliest times, the community of monks and nuns, or the *sangha*, has formed the central core of the Buddhist religion.

In Theravada countries the monks (there are really very few nuns) are called *bhikkhus* and are easy to recognize because they wear orange-coloured robes, shave their heads and walk about either barefoot or in sandals.

Young people may first join a monastery at a fairly early age. If after that, having talked the matter over with their teachers, they decide that the life is

Below *Monks and nuns at prayer in a temple in Thailand.*

other hand, there has been a steady increase in the number of Buddhists to be found in the West, where many people, perhaps disenchanted with violence, greed and the endless quest for wealth, have been attracted by the teachings of the Buddha. It has been estimated that there are now over 10,000 practising native Buddhists in Britain.

right for them, then they commit themselves to the *sangha* by becoming fully ordained. They are then given a new Buddhist name and are bound to live by a very strict code of rules called the *Vinaya*.

Bhikkhus live simple, disciplined lives. Most of their time is taken up by meditation, chanting and perhaps, when they are sufficiently experienced, some teaching. They will also go out daily on an alms-round, carrying begging-bowls so that kind lay people can give them food. They are only allowed one meal a day and that should be taken before noon. As they are not allowed to marry, go to entertainments,

A young Burmese boy has his head shaved before his initiation as a monk.

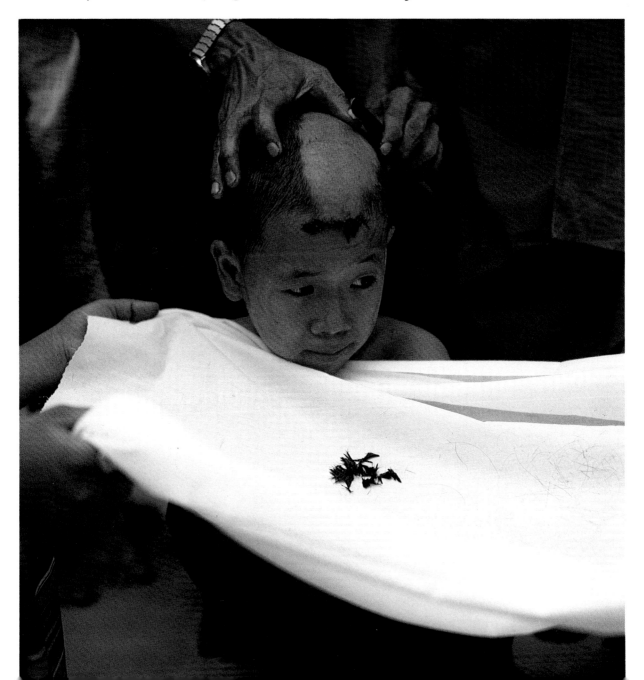

own many possessions nor, in the case of the strictest of them, carry money, you can appreciate that it is a pretty hard life, appealing only to those with a very strong sense of dedication to following the Buddha's teachings. To make things even more tough, they are only allowed very short hours of sleep.

Monks are also to be found in Mahayana countries, although not in the same numbers that they used to be. They too cannot marry and must live according to a certain code of rules.

Tibetan monks prepare tsampa, *the simple food which makes up the main part of their diet.*

The rules do, however, differ from the *Vinaya* of Theravada monks and are generally less strict. Japanese Zen monks will, for instance, drink *sake* (rice wine) and carry money. Like their Chinese counterparts in years gone by, they may also spend rather more time working to support themselves than Theravada *bhikkhus* do.

Monks outside a temple in Hong Kong. Monastery rules tend to be less strict in Mahayanan countries than in Theravada ones.

Ceremonies and Customs

Buddhist festivals

There is a wide variety of ways in which Buddhists celebrate their religion, and these tend to differ from country to country. The most important events in the life of the Buddha, such as his birth, his discovery of *nirvana* and his death, are, however, celebrated by Buddhists everywhere.

Many of the oldest Buddhist festivals

Monks are nearly always at the forefront of any major festival.

are celebrated at times of the year which are important to monks. In Thailand, for instance, a festival called *Kathina* is held at the end of a three-month period of study and meditation in the monastic calendar. At *Kathina*, lay people express their thanks to monks by giving them gifts of food, drink and cloth for their robes.

Wesak, or *Vaisakha,* is another major Theravada festival, at which the birth, enlightenment and death of the Buddha are celebrated.

Some festivals celebrate Buddhist teachers of the past and times of seasonal change, such as New Year, whereas others are focused on one particular place. It may be a place of

pilgrimage or the site of some famous religious relic. During the *Esala Perahera,* which is held each year in Sri Lanka, there is a magnificent torchlight procession through the town of Kandy. A tooth which is said to have belonged to the Buddha is carried through the streets on the back of a magnificently costumed elephant, as the people looking on joyfully celebrate their religion.

Below *Gyantse Monastery in Tibet. Many Buddhist festivals are held to mark significant events in the monastic calendar.*

Above *A procession taking place during the* Esala Perahera.

Rites of passage

Like their festivals, Buddhists' birth, marriage and death ceremonies vary from tradition to tradition and from country to country. Despite this variation, nearly all the ceremonies involve the participation of Buddhist monks.

In Theravada Buddhist countries, for instance, parents will take a new-born child along to their local temple so that it may be given a Buddhist name. The

Monks are given food after attending a cremation ceremony in Thailand.

baby is also sprinkled with water and blessed, to ensure a happy future life. Finally, a candle of pure wax is burned so that the molten droplets fall into a bowl of pure water. This symbolizes the coming together of the four elements: earth, air, fire and water.

In Theravada marriage ceremonies, a thread made of cotton is passed around the statue of the Buddha upon the temple shrine and then around all the people present, including the monks. After some chanting and the giving of a blessing, two pieces are cut from this thread. One is tied around the wrist of the

bridegroom by the senior monk present and then the bridegroom ties the second piece around his wife's wrist. The bridegroom does this because Buddhist monks are forbidden to touch women. These pieces of thread, which symbolize the union into which the man and woman have entered, should be worn until they drop off naturally.

Finally, when anyone dies, Theravada Buddhist monks will chant daily for twelve days. Then, at the funeral itself, there will be a special ceremony at which everyone present transfers their good merit to the dead person so that he or she may have a fortunate rebirth. The transfer of merit is symbolized by pouring water from a ewer into two bowls placed one inside the other. Finally, as the dead person is being cremated (cremation is usual among Buddhists of the southern tradition), there will be further chanting.

All these ceremonies are accompanied by the giving of offerings (*dana*) by the lay people to the monks taking part in the ceremony.

Monks in ceremonial robes conduct a funeral service in Ladakh.

Arts and Artefacts

A Buddhist shrine

Most Buddhists will make a shrine somewhere in their homes. A typical one will have a statue, or *buddharupa,* in pride of place. In front of the statue, there will usually be some kind of holder in which sweet-smelling incense can be burned, and nearby, there will be a store of candles. Buddhists light candles on their shrines to symbolize the light that the Buddha's great wisdom brought into the world. Burning incense, on the other hand, is a way of showing devotion and also of producing a pleasant atmosphere in which meditation or some kind of ceremony can take place.

Finally the shrine will be decorated with vases of flowers. This is all that is basically necessary, but people can put other offerings there if they wish or if their particular tradition prefers it. Tibetan Buddhists, for instance, place bowls of fresh water on their shrines. They may even place food there as an offering to the Buddha, as well as texts wrapped up in silk, and miniature *stupas.*

Vases of flowers decorate this miniature shrine in a Japanese monastery. Inside the shrine is a buddharupa — *a small statue of the Buddha.*

A Japanese woman lights a holy candle at her local shrine.

The gold roof of the Shwedagon Pagoda in Rangoon, Burma.

Temples, monasteries and stupas

Religious buildings, many of them very grand and splendid, are to be found — or at least were once to be found — in all Buddhist countries. They are often elaborately decorated and filled with works of art of an extremely high order.

The basic Buddhist structure is a simple temple or meeting house which contains a shrine upon which a *buddharupa* is placed. Religious ceremonies and meditation sessions are conducted here. Attached to the building may be accommodation facilities for a number of monks. These temple-monastery complexes range in size from the humble to the colossal: Drepung Monastery in Tibet housed almost 8,000 monks at one time.

Another important structure in Buddhism is the *stupa* or *pagoda*. Originally, *stupas* were built over relics of the Buddha, but more people wanted to build *stupas* than there were relics to go round. As a result, statues, sacred writings and other blessed objects were put inside *stupas* and sealed up. You can't enter a *stupa*; it is just a monument to commemorate the Buddha and his teachings. While most of them are quite small, the largest, which is to be found at the famous Shwedagon Temple in Burma, is some 113 metres (370 feet) tall and is encased in gold leaf. Another fantastically colossal *stupa* is to be found at Borobodur in Indonesia.

Buddhist monuments at the ancient site of Pagan in Burma.

The Jataka Tales

The Jataka Tales are a collection of over 500 stories said to have been told by Gautama the Buddha to his followers. As an illustration of what these tales are like, here is Jataka 36:

The Burning Tree

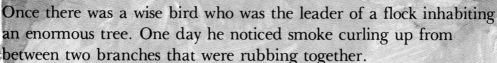

Once there was a wise bird who was the leader of a flock inhabiting an enormous tree. One day he noticed smoke curling up from between two branches that were rubbing together.

'If that continues this tree will catch fire,' he warned his fellow birds. 'And the fire will easily spread to these dry old leaves. Then the whole tree will blaze up and burn to the ground. The sensible thing to do is leave straight away and go to a safer place.'

The wiser birds in the flock followed their leader's advice and flew away to a safe place with him. There were other, foolish birds, however, who took no notice and stayed where they were.

In a very short time and just as the wise bird had predicted, the tree caught fire. The foolish birds dropped off the branches into the flames and were destroyed, thus paying the penalty for failing to heed wise advice.

43

Conclusion

Like all the great world religions, Buddhism has become very complicated. It has a vast amount of scriptures (the largest number of any religion); it has countless temples, monasteries and shrines; and it has divided up into innumerable groups and sub-groups, each with its own particular interpretation of the teachings, its own practices and its own rituals. Yet amidst all this diversity, Buddhists everywhere look back to the historical Buddha as the originator and founder of their practices, and to his simple experience of the truth as the core or heart of their religion.

Buddhist culture is as colourful as it is varied.

In Buddhism, no one is left out, for the deeper nature that the Buddha found, the origin of all goodness, wisdom and life, is in everyone, even if they don't know it. He did not wish people to believe in him or worship him, but rather for them to find this precious jewel for themselves. It is not something that is only to be found in distant lands, or that has to be manufactured. The veils of ignorance and confusion in our minds have merely to be drawn back for truth to be revealed in all its splendour.

For all its regional differences, Buddhism is ultimately a religion founded on the basic truths expounded by the Buddha himself.

The countries and regions of eastern Asia in which Buddhism is, or has been, a major religious force.

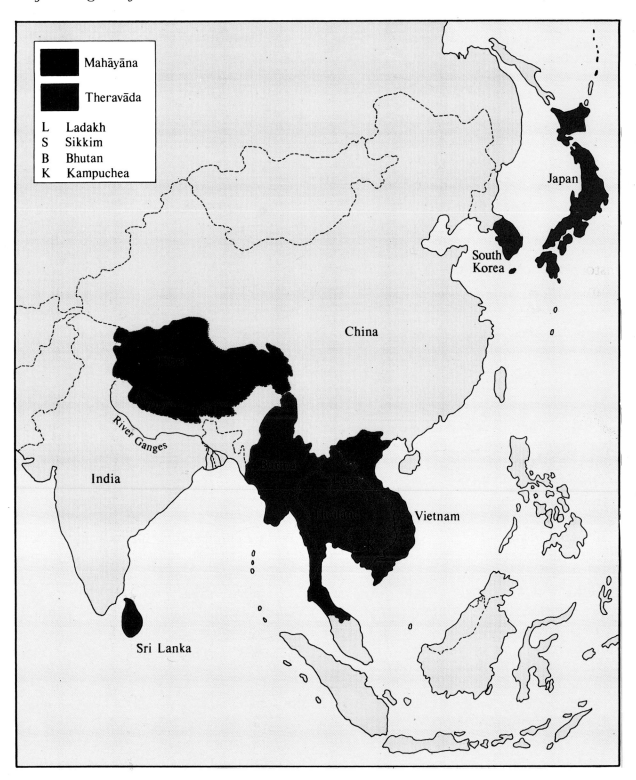

Glossary

The Buddha's teachings were first written down in two ancient Indian languages, Pali and Sanskrit. Theravada Buddhists tend to use Pali, Mahayana Buddhists Sanskrit. In this glossary, Pali terms are identified by (P), Sanskrit terms by (Skt).

Anatta The lack, as the Buddha saw it, of any permanent underlying self or soul.

Anicca Change. One of the Three Signs of Being.

Arhat (Skt), **Arahat** (P) A person who has followed the Buddha's Way to the end and entered *nirvana*.

Bhikkhu A Buddhist monk.

Bodhisattva (Skt), **Bodhisatta** (P) A person who could enter *nirvana*, but who puts it off in order to stay in the world and help suffering beings.

Bo tree (Bodhi tree) The tree beneath which the Buddha gained his enlightenment.

Buddha 'The Awakened One'; the title given to Siddhartha Gautama after his enlightenment.

Buddharupa A statue of the Buddha.

Dharma (Skt), **Dhamma** (P) The teachings of the Buddha.

Dukkha Suffering or discomfort; a general sense of unsatisfactoriness.

Esala Perahera A major Buddhist festival in Sri Lanka.

Karma (Skt), **Kamma** (P) The law of cause and effect which indicates that any willed action will produce an appropriate result. A good action produces a good result, a bad action a bad one.

Jataka Tales A collection of over 500 stories which are said to have been told by the Buddha.

Kathina A Theravada festival in which cloth and other useful things are given by lay people to monks.

Mahayana The later school of Buddhism which takes the *bodhisattva* as its ideal and which flourished in central, northern and eastern Asian countries.

Nirvana (Skt), **Nibbana** (P) Literally a 'blowing out' or extinction, as of a candle. *Nirvana,* the final goal of Buddhism, is reached when all greed, hatred and delusion are set to rest and there is no longer any desire.

Parinirvana (Skt), **Parinibbana** (P) The final or ultimate *nirvana* that the Buddha entered upon his death.

Sangha The community of Buddhist monks and nuns.

Sila Morality, or a kind of Buddhist code of conduct.

Stupa Originally burial mounds, *stupas* have developed into characteristic Buddhist monuments, taking various forms in various countries.

Theravada Sometimes called the Southern School because it is mainly found in southeast Asian countries. This school takes the *arahat,* as opposed to the *bodhisattva,* as its ideal.

Vinaya The code of discipline by which Buddhist monks must live.

Zen A Japanese school of Mahayana Buddhism laying great stress on meditation.

Books to Read

A Short History of Buddhism by Edward Conze (Allen & Unwin, 1980)

Buddhism by Christmas Humphreys (Pelican, 1951)

Buddhist Festivals by John Snelling (Wayland, 1985)

Buddhists and Buddhism by Martha Patrick (Wayland, 1984)

Ten Buddhist Fables by John Snelling (Buddhist Publication Group, 1984)

The Buddhist World by Anne Bancroft (MacDonald, 1984)

The Life of the Buddha by H. Saddhatissa (Allen & Unwin, 1976)

The World of Buddhism ed. H. Bechert & R. Gombrich (Thames & Hudson, 1984)

Tibet, Land of Snows by Giuseppe Tucci (Elek, 1967)

Most of the above books may be obtained by mail order from: Knightsbridge Books, 32 Store Street, London WC1E 7BS, England.

Acknowledgements

The publisher would like to thank all those who provided the illustrations on the following pages: Camerapix Hutchison Library 5 *(top)*, 14 *(top)*, 29 *(top)*, 33; J. Allan Cash Photolibrary *front cover;* Bruce Coleman Ltd 4 (Sandro Prato), 16, 39, 44 *(left)* (Jaroslav Poncar), 18 (L. C. Marigo), 21 (Jonathan Wright); Colorpix 10, 17, 32 *(right)*, 42; Geoscience Features 11, 19, 34, 36; Christopher Gibb 13, 28, 31, 37 *(bottom)*; Francis D. Leather 41 *(left);* Outlook Films Ltd 5 *(bottom)*, 7, 9, 20, 22, 24, 25, 32 *(left)*, 38, 40, 44 *(right);* Ann & Bury Peerless 6, 8, 12, 41 *(right);* Sri Lankan Tourist Board 14 *(bottom)*, 15, 23, 26, 29 *(bottom)*, 30 *(left)*, 30 *(right)*, 37 *(top);* TOPHAM 27; Malcolm Walker 12, 43, 45; Wayland Picture Library 35.

Index